To Compostela and Beyond!

To Compostela and Beyond!

A Poet's Chronicle of the Camino de Santiago

Susana Porras

Foreword by Thelma T. Reyna

RESOURCE *Publications* · Eugene, Oregon

TO COMPOSTELA AND BEYOND!
A Poet's Chronicle of the Camino de Santiago

Resource Publications
An Imprint of Wipf and Stock Publishers
199 W. 8th Ave., Suite 3
Eugene, OR 97401

www.wipfandstock.com

PAPERBACK ISBN: 978-1-7252-8760-0
HARDCOVER ISBN: 978-1-7252-8759-4
EBOOK ISBN: 978-1-7252-8761-7

02/01/21

This book is dedicated to Axcel and Tomasa
who have dedicated their entire lives to their only child, me!

Each step you take reveals a new horizon.
You have taken the first step today.
Now, I challenge you to take another.

—DAN POYNTER

Contents

Foreword

WITHIN THESE PAGES, SUSANA Porras has created an exceptional collection of poems detailing the 500-mile physical and spiritual journey she undertook with her 73-year-old father along the historic Camino de Santiago in the summer of 2018. Originally inspired from her daily travel diary, these poems celebrate herein the beauties and wonders of the European nations she traversed on foot in a trek most people would be too faint-hearted to undertake.

Over their 32-day trip, Susana and her father walked 10, 15, sometimes even 20 miles each day! As you will read, they experienced both the stunning natural beauties of Spain and the warmth of the Spaniards: their food, hospitality, authenticity. They also became closer than ever as father and daughter.

Within the eight chapters of this book (each one representing a different geographic region of Spain as their journey progressed), Susana takes us from their beginnings at the crowded airport, converging with other pilgrims on the trail, through the practicalities of taking care of blisters, and on to the culinary delights they tasted; all while appreciating the stunning panoramas and vistas of natural beauty.

Taken together, the 39 poems are gentle, reflective, honest, and disciplined. Even for an experienced poet, writing a Shakespearean sonnet is difficult. To describe a life-changing journey entirely in sonnets, as Susana has done, is a unique and marvelous feat. Poet lovers, fans of travel writings, and people who cherish spiritual poetry have a gift here that will delight and inspire.

Thelma T. Reyna, PhD
Author of *Dearest Papa:*
A Memoir in Poems

Acknowledgements

We value the sage and sound advice
For our journey of reflective thought.
It brought to our lives an inner peace
That for several decades, we keenly sought.

To our most dearest family and friends,
You were with us every step of the way.
Your love and prayers tied the loosened ends
Of our mission each and every day.

You who provided input to this book
With loads of special gifts and complex skills.
A number of you gave a second look,
Sufficient to provide the added thrill.

However, this is not our final stop,
Explore with us on our next country hop!

Introduction

June 1, 2018: I landed in Biarritz Airport in France with my 73-year-old father. I had spent the past nine months researching and planning and—finally—here we were, about to embark on a life-changing adventure. The Camino de Santiago had been calling me for eight years, and now we were going to spend the next 32 days walking and hiking over five hundred miles together.

If you are reading this, you are at the very least curious about the Camino, you may have already walked it, or you may be in the process of planning your own journey of self-discovery. My goal with this book is to inspire you to make the trek yourself, whether for spiritual awakening, health reasons, or simply to take pleasure in the beauty and majesty of the Camino de Santiago.

For those who aren't familiar with the Camino de Santiago (or "Way of Saint James"), travelers can begin their journey from different starting points in different countries, with all routes converging into one at the end. My father and I chose the French Way. This is the original route used continuously since 812 AD by religious pilgrims on their way to visit the shrine of the Apostle Saint James the Great in the Cathedral of Santiago de Compostela in northwestern Spain.

Before embarking on our journey, I studied a variety of books, videos, and articles about the Camino. My favorite and primary resource for this trip was John Brierley's book *A Pilgrim's Guide to the Camino de Santiago: St. Jean—Roncesvalles—Santiago*. I booked small pensions and hotels at many of Brierley's recommended stops, and the 39 sonnets herein reflect most of those suggested stages: roaming through the Spanish provinces of Navarra, La Rioja, Burgos, Palencia, León, Lugo, and La Coruña, and highlighting the contrasting physical geography of the regions, including a majestic mountain range, sun-pelted plains, and storybook woodlands.

The Camino as a metaphor of life was a recurring theme during the pilgrimage my father and I took along the Camino de Santiago. Several pilgrims walked or cycled straight through, the more adventurous sought paths with higher levels of difficulty, and others stopped to enjoy the numerous sites along the way, unhindered by self-created deadlines.

Along with my father, my companions on this trip were a tiny orange notebook and an even tinier pen. Inspiration would be all around me, and I wanted to document it each day. After much thought, I'd chosen poetry, specifically the Shakespearean sonnet, as my way to chronicle this journey and share it with others. They say a picture is worth a thousand words—and I took a lot of them!—but the challenge of creating that same picture with less than a hundred words arranged into 14 ten-syllable lines . . . challenge accepted!

At their most rudimentary level, these sonnets are my impression of the Camino and the unforgettable experiences my father and I shared. For those who wish to look deeper, they also include some of the region's varied history and the treasures my father and I discovered when deviating from the waymarked route. May these sonnets inspire you to memorialize your own experiences and to pray, meditate, and explore. Buen Camino!

1

US/France

Sonnet 1: Home—Pasadena, California USA

May 30, 2018

The eve of our well-prepared retreat,
A farewell dinner spread for mom and friends.
A time to laugh, connect, and pass the sweets,
And share my dream to reach the western end.[1]

Specific questions I have answers for,
Amid all, I acknowledge every doubt.
My simple story grows as local lore.
And wonder if it's bright or bleak throughout.

The Wednesday night social draws to a close.
We hug, we kiss, and say, see you later.
The gracious ritual everyone knows.
Love and friends, almost nothing is greater.

I turn and gesture one last wave goodbye,
Taking one last glimpse at the night's blue sky.

---

1. Brierley, *A Pilgrim's Guide*, 280. "Western" refers to Finisterre, an area once believed to be the end of the world, and is now the final destination for many Camino pilgrims.

3

Sonnet 2: First Steps

May 31, 2018

I ponder what appears an endless path,
Where beauty, nature, and color abounds.
All scheming to conceal the certain wrath.
My thoughts contrive and wonder, my heart pounds.

Beyond the threshold to the vast unknown.
I take a breath and few initial steps.
A final scavenge for a burden stone.[1]
I stop to question several months of prep.

We covered items on essentials list,[2]
To ensure our journey's grand success.
A little worried about practice missed,
Assured however of the skills possessed.

I compose myself and collect my rock,
Then pursue our quest to connect the dots.

---

1. Brierley, *A Pilgrim's Guide*, 210. A "Burden stone," is a small rock that carries a special meaning for the pilgrim and is traditionally placed at the base of the Cruz de Ferro (Sonnet 30).

2. See appendix for packing essentials.

Sonnet 3: On the Way to Paris

May 31, 2018—June 1, 2018

Our trip stalls in the afternoon gridlock.
We sit quietly, not saying a word,
And arrive a quarter past three o'clock,
Just in time to check in and join the herd.

We walk by the mugs and kitschy keychains,
Past throngs of selfie-obsessed globetrotters,
To a view of perfectly aligned planes.
One will fly us across open waters.

I take a peek through the cabin window,
Anticipating the powerful thrust.
I close my eyes and adjust my pillow,
All my faith in the pilot I entrust.

Enticed to stay in the City of Light,[1]
But best to take the next connecting flight.

1. Steves, *Paris 2008*, 1. Paris is also known as the City of Lights.

Sonnet 4: On the Way to Biarritz

June 1, 2018

We step out of the plane and back in time
To the charm of the pearl of the Basque coast.
Summer breeze, salty air—simply sublime,
But it is the sunshine I enjoy most.

We pause to sample the local cuisine
At a bistro[1] overlooking the sea.
The shimmery water blue and pristine,
Of this enchanted place that came to be.

Playground of surfers and celebrities[2]
All sunbathing on the sandy beaches.
Classic-striped tents of the 1920's
By and large, the most sought after niches.

The sun begins to set above the seas,
Appearing glad to move with slothful ease.

1. Restaurant Le Bistrot Sainte Cluque 9 Rue Hugues, 64100 Bayonne, France. It is necessary to explain that my friend Manou picked us up from the airport in Biarritz, gave us a guided tour of the town, and drove us to Bayonne, where he treated us to a nice dinner.

2. Marsh, *French Atlantic Coast*, 208. Biarritz is a beautiful seaside town that has attracted surfers, celebrities, and royals for decades.

Sonnet 5: On the Way to Saint-Jean-Pied-de-Port

June 2, 2018

Saint-Jean-Pied-de-Port[1] is our starting place
To check in and secure a passport doc[2]
And extra food and supplies, just in case
We failed to purchase some essential stock.

Quaint village of winding cobblestone streets,
That boasts sun-dried pepper-colored shutters.
The typical "buen camino"[3] that greets,
In transit pilgrims searching waymarkers.[4]

The River Nive[5] runs through this little town
An offshoot of the Ardour waterway.[6]
Slow foot traffic from sunup to sundown
Of hikers who began the walk in May.

1. Kurlansky, *The Basque History*, 28. Saint-Jean-Pied-de-Port is a French Basque town on the border of Spain at the base of the Pyrenees Mountains.

2. Brierley, *A Pilgrim's Guide*, 44. "Passport doc (document)" refers to the traditional pilgrim passport obtained at the Pilgrim Welcome Office in Saint-Jean-Pied-de-Port, 39 Rue de la Citadelle, 64220 Saint-Jean-Pied-de-Port, France. https://stjeanpieddeport-roncevaux.jimdofree.com/english/pilgrims-office/

3. Steves, *Spain 2016*, 252. The customary pilgrim greeting is "*Buen camino*," or "Happy travels."

4. Brierley, *A Pilgrim's Guide*, 39. *Waymarkers*, traditionally in the form of yellow arrows, are placed by volunteers as directional signage for Camino pilgrims.

5. Brierley, *A Pilgrim's Guide*, 50. The River Nive runs through Saint-Jean-Pied-de-Port.

6. Kurlansky, *The Basque History*, 18. The Ardour River flows to the Atlantic Ocean near Bayonne, France where the Basque region begins.

With scallop shell[7]and office stamp in hand,
We set off to explore this sacred land.

7. Steves, *Spain 2017*, 268. The Scallop shell is the most popular symbol of the Camino de Santiago and it is tradition for Pilgrims to carry one tied to their belongings.

2

Navarra

Sonnet 6: On the Way to Roncesvalles

June 3, 2018—24 km (14.9 mi.)

We made it today through Roncevaux Pass,[1]
A trail of mountains tying France and Spain.[2]
A challenge for the agile to surpass,
One summit conquered, many more remain.

We stop to admire the birds-eye view
Of this blissful and legendary place.
Difficult to fathom beyond the blue,
The tragedy that occurred in this space.

The Basque ambush of Charlemagne's[3] rear guard,
In the Song of Roland[4] forever etched.
The Frankish[5] army battled long and hard
But in reality was far outstretched.

1. Kurlansky, *The Basque History*, 40. Ronceveaux Pass is the French name for Roncesvalles Pass in Spanish, and translates to the place where the pine trees grow. Ronceveaux Pass is a narrow passage in the Pyrenees Mountains between France and Spain.

2. Steves, *Spain 2017*, 261–62. The Pyrenees Mountain range separates the Iberian Peninsula from the rest of Europe.

3. Brierley, *A Pilgrim's Guide*, 54. Charlemagne, also known as Charles the Great, held several crowns, including that of king of the Franks from 768.

4. O'Halloran et al., *Essential Spain*, 370. The Battle of Roncevaux in 778 AD was the catalyst for the creation of France's most famous epic poem, *The Song of Roland*. Charlemagne's rear guard, under the direction of his nephew Roland, was decimated by Basque soldiers.

5. Brierley, *A Pilgrim's Guide*, 31. "Frankish," refers to the Franks, a Germanic tribe that migrated from northern Europe and settled in Francia, part of what we know today as modern day France.

Tale told on scores of impromptu stages[6]
Of kings and knights of the Middle Ages.

6. Paterson, *The World of the Troubadours,* 1. "Impromptu stages," is
suggestive of the troubadours, traveling performers of the Middle Ages, who
recited poetry, among other forms of entertainment.

Sonnet 7: On the Way to Zubiri

June 4, 2018—22 km (13.7 mi.)

News of the eruption arrived this morn,
Of the volcano[1] near my mother's home,
The hamlet[2] of her youth where she was born,
A place where dogs and children safely roam.

We made many frantic calls, but no word
From any of our friends or relatives.
Still shocked to hear the latest harm incurred,
We forget other clear imperatives.

Accepting our current helpless state,
In silence, we assemble our things.
Ahead, the march continues passed estates,
Across translucent water spewing springs.

We finally breathe a sigh of relief
From the message, "she is fine," we receive.

---

1. Wallace, "The Guatemala Volcano Eruption," lines 1—4. The Volcano of Fire erupted in Guatemala, Central America on Sunday, June 3, 2018.

2. "The hamlet" refers to Quisaché, Chimaltenango in Guatemala, Central America.

Sonnet 8: On the Way to Pamplona

June 5, 2018—19 km (11.8 mi.)

The peaceful tranquility of our walk,
Shattered by the bustle of modern life.
We gather with new friends and make small talk
About the region's political strife.[1]

We do as Hemingway[2] and his friends did,
But opt for coffee instead of red wine
And find pleasure in staying off the grid
As we hear tales more engaging than mine.

We run and dodge imaginary bulls,[3]
The unnerving feeling of facing death,
The slight chance of being trampled by hooves,
The warm, moist, forceful exhale of their breath.

We leave our handkerchiefs[4] and grab our poles
To put more kilometers on our souls.

1. Steves, *Spain,* 170–72. "The region's political strife," refers to decades of Basques' struggle for independence from Spain.

2. Dearborn, *Ernest Hemingway,* 189. American author, Ernest Hemingway loved Pamplona, visited often, and wrote about it in his 1926 novel, *The Sun Also Rises.*

3. O'Halloran et al., *Fodor's Essential Spain,* 312. The tradition of the running of the bulls occurs every year the week of July 6 during the Festival of San Fermín in Pamplona, Spain.

4. Steves, *Spain 2017,* 270–71. "Handkerchiefs" refers to the red scarves that *Running of the Bulls* participants traditionally wear around their necks.

Sonnet 9: On the Way to Puente la Reina

June 6, 2018—24 km (14.9 mi.)

It is ever so dismaying to see
Backpackers racing on Camino trails;
As though running from a swarming bee,
Ignoring Mother Nature's lush details.

Every shrub boasts a colorful bouquet,
All striking, delicate, and beautiful.
Greeting pilgrims every step of the way,
The sweet chirping sounds of birds bountiful.

We opt for a detour on a side street
To the octagonal Romanesque church,[1]
Unknowingly with blisters on my feet.
Worth it to see the fruits of my research.

We enjoy every moment of the way
And prepare to do the same the next day.

---

1. Brierley, *A Pilgrim's Guide*, 72. Iglesia de Santa María de Eunate, s/n, 31152 Muruzábal, Navarra, Spain. http://santamariadeeunate.es/

Sonnet 10: On the Way to Estella

June 7, 2018—21 km (13.0 mi.)

Today we walked on ancient Roman roads[1]
Through medieval towns of stone and timber
With links to the Knights Templar's[2] secret codes
And whose treasures are believed to shimmer.

Whole landscapes blanketed with poppy fields,
Fertile plantations of grape-bearing vines,
All producing unparalleled crop yields
That will soon be processed into fine wines.

The rain begins cascading life anew
Within an hour rural lands are quenched.
Degrees have dropped and walking pilgrims few,
It's no surprise that both of us are drenched.

But late this afternoon, the sun shone bright,
And gave us strength to continue the plight.

1. Brierley, *A Pilgrim's Guide*, 78.
2. Brierley, *A Pilgrim's Guide,* 76–78. The small village of Mañeru Centro has historical links to the Knights Templar and Order of St. John.

Sonnet 11: On the Way to Los Arcos

June 8, 2018—20 km (12.4 mi.)

This latest stage propels us to a line
With other pilgrims waiting for a taste.
The Bodegas Irache[1] ruby wine,
Behind a public fountain source encased.

Over a small hill and to our surprise,
Under the pleasant shade of two birch trees,
The sweet sound of tango beneath the skies.
Two folk musicians playing in the breeze.

Band-Aids, bandages, nor layers of socks
Had brought respite to my two injured feet.
With countless remaining steps over rocks,
I whispered the Lord's Prayer,[2] short and sweet.

Perhaps celestial fate or stroke of luck,
I'm able to continue our walk.

---

1. Brierley, *A Pilgrim's Guide*, 86. Bodegas Irache kindly offers pilgrims a free sample of their wine via an outdoor fountain. Wine Fountain at Bodegas Irache Camino de Santiago, 91A, 31240 Ayegui, Navarra, Spain. https://www.irache.com

2. Luke 11:2–4 (New International Version).

3

La Rioja

.

Sonnet 12: On the Way to Logroño

June 9, 2018—28.4 km (17.6 mi.)

Beneath an olive tree, we find a priest
Applying dressings to his injured feet.
His walk appears to have completely ceased,
But hobbles onward to a steady beat.

Advancing strongly with an even pace
Provides a unique moment to reboot.
Inside the packed canteen,[1] we share a space
Before resuming the remaining route.

Departing we're perplexed by playful jeers
From prudent hikers waiting break of day.
My father quickly waves to our peers
Who shout inspiring blessings for the way.

On arrival, we are met by revelers
And can't help but join the feasting dwellers.[2]

---

1. Café RUA, Calle Rúa Santa María, 8, 31230 Viana Spain.

2. Ham et al., *Lonely Planet Spain*, 448. The Feast of San Bernabé (Saint Barnabas), celebrated in Logroño, Spain on June 11, commemorates the victory and resistance against French invaders in 1521.

Sonnet 13: On the Way to Nájera

June 10, 2018—27 km (16.8 mi.)

Revived by espresso and apple pie,[1]
We seek another part of our trek.
We pass a lake of carp[2] abruptly spry
For morsels tossed by children safe on deck.

At Alto de la Grajera,[3] we pause
Above a noisy traffic laden spot,
Where makeshift crosses dangle for a cause.
My father places one within a slot.

It feels, by far, to be the longest day.
Exhaustion hits two pairs of well-worn feet.
The target seems like endless miles away,
Again enticed to find an empty seat.

A trotter shows compassion for our pain
And slows to pace we're able to maintain.

---

1. Cafetería Mónaco, Calle Marqués de Murrieta, 28, Bajo, 26005 Logroño, La Rioja, Spain.

2. Brierley, *A Pilgrim's Guide* 100. Grajera Park Pantano de la Grajera, s/n, 26007 Logroño, La Rioja, Spain.

3. Brierley, *A Pilgrim's Guide,* 100.

Sonnet 14: On the Way to Santo Domingo de la Calzada

June 11, 2018—20 km (12.4 mi.)

Afflicted with another blister woe,
Including many partly mended sores.
Resolving to relax and take it slow,
We take advantage of the great outdoors.

Along the road, a lone commanding mast.[1]
Intrigued observers, one by one, draw near.
They probe the offbeat totem from the past
Intent on making their assumptions clear.

Bewildered by the broken cross-like post,
We also question its intended use.
A local knows the gruesome story most,
Of felons who endured their last abuse.

Today's discomfort now a distant thought,
Instead, we think about the lessons taught.

1. Brierley, *A Pilgrim's Guide*, 106 and 110. Mast refers to gallows. This distinctive column served as the town's border and in the medieval period was a place where sentences were carried out. This stone column is in Azofra, Spain between Nájera and Santo Domingo de la Calzada.

4

Castilla y León (Burgos)

Sonnet 15: On the Way to Belorado

June 12, 2018—22 km (13.7 mi.)

Ominous grey clouds block the vast blue sky.
The morning is chilly, damp, and windy.
Traversing hamlets where time doesn't fly,
Heirs of structures that appear quite flimsy.

Stopping a moment at a hip café,[1]
We share achievement goals and battle scars.
The ballads of Billie Holiday[2] play,
As well as those of other big jazz stars.

Walking along, we come across a sign,
A common yellow arrow waymarker
Stating the distance to the finish line:
Still five hundred kilometers farther.

We take one more look and snap a photo
And continue walking through the meadow.

---

1. Bar "My Way," Plaza de la Iglesia, 4, 26259 Grañón, La Rioja, Spain. https://www.mywayfrances.com/

2. Szwed, *Billie Holiday*, 3. Billie Holiday was a renowned African-American jazz singer in the early 20th century.

Sonnet 16: On the Way to Atapuerca

June 13, 2018—29 km (18.0 mi.)

Placed on the Paseo del Ánimo[1]
The classic format of Grauman's Chinese,[2]
A custom American pilgrims know,
Prints produced by stars on their hands and knees.

We make a stop at a garden café,[3]
A welcome respite from the prolonged walk.
Although the consequence is a delay,
We all make it a point to sit and talk.

Again misjudging footpath length and climb,
We picture rather late the lone approach.
A sure arrival under darkened skies,
A daunting topic neither wants to broach.

A more secluded yet rewarding hike,
We notice very little we dislike.

1. Celebrity hand and footprint impressions on the "Paseo del Ánimo," can be found on the following streets in Belorado, Spain la calle Mayor, la calle Raimundo de Miguel y Navas, and la calle Hipólito López Bernal.

2. Wanamaker, *Hollywood: 1940—2008*, 182–83. TCL Chinese Theatre, 6925 Hollywood Blvd, Hollywood, CA 90028. http://www.tclchinesetheatres. com/

3. Albergue Los Arancones Bar, Tosantos calle de la Iglesia s/n Burgos, Spain.

Sonnet 17: On the Way to Burgos

June 14, 2018—18 km (11.2 mi.)

We arose to a path of solid stone,
To a vista of the valley below,
Of a village[1] painted in the same tone,
A classic Spanish countryside tableau.

We often look for a familiar face,
But see none of our friends on the trails.
It's been difficult to keep the same pace
On this pilgrimage, that so much entails.

The daily trek is always a challenge,
The last remaining steps are most severe.
I'm often tempted to leave the baggage
However, steadfast pilgrims carry gear.

Late this eve, we are pleasantly surprised
When we see our friends with our own two eyes.

---

1. Brierley, *A Pilgrim's Guide*, 127. "Village" refers to Villalval, the first small town visible from La Cruz de Matagrande.

Sonnet 18: On the Way to Hornillos del Camino

June 15, 2018—20 km (12.4 mi.)

Leaving town, we visit a hermitage[1]
Where we are greeted by a gracious guide,
Who shares the benevolent heritage
Of caring for pilgrims at their bedside.

We start the walk on the immense plateau,[2]
A place alleged to be intense and bare.
We thought it would be best to keep it slow
And take a recess from the pelting glare.

The gravel road embraced by fields of wheat
Bestows the pilgrim with fantastic views,
But offers no protection from the heat.
Degrees begin to rise beneath our shoes.

The day ends with a grand communal feast.
The tender roasted pork loin lasts the least.[3]

---

1. Brierley, *A Pilgrim's Guide*, 136. Ermita de San Amaro, University of Burgos Calle San Amaro, s/n, 09001 Burgos, Spain.

2. Brierley, *A Pilgrim's Guide,* 134–35. The *meseta* or Spanish plateau is an area of flat plains in Spain that is about 220 km long.

3. Hotel Rural La Consulta de Isar Calle Real, 27, 09653 Isar, Burgos Spain.

Sonnet 19: On the Way to Castrojeriz

June 16, 2018—21 km (13.0 mi.)

Assorted flowers line the dusty way,
Enticing many birds and butterflies.
All are enjoying the wonderful display
Of red and purple blossoms, earth provides.

We stumble upon the ancient ruins
Of San Anton's[1] hospice and monastery,
Known for the Tau[2] and good they were doing,
Saw healing through love as necessary.

Around a corner, we explore a farm
And find the owner tending to his stock.
The homestead brimming with intrinsic charm.
We chat then gesture adieu to the flock.

By chance, we stumble on a longer route,
Instead, we laugh and make a friend to boot!

1. Brierley, *A Pilgrim's Guide*, 143.
2. Brierley, *A Pilgrim's Guide*, 143.

5

Castilla y León (Palencia)

Sonnet 20: On the Way to Frómista

June 17, 2018—24 km (14.0 mi.)

The morning begins with a long, steep climb
To a grand view of the patchwork plateau.
Squares in shades of berries, lemons, and limes
Are perfectly placed on the ground below.

At the summit[1], we take a break with friends
To take advantage of the photo op.
A few minutes later, the group descends,
And turns to take a picture of the top.

After lunch, we are a little sluggish—
And the sun calls for a nap, not a walk.
We see a friend cycling to the finish.
To see him racing on wheels is a shock.

Upon exchanging stories, we part ways.
Perchance we'll see him in another phase.

1. Brierley, *A Pilgrim's Guide*, 148. "Summit" refers to the observation deck
at Alto de Mosterales. Camino Francés, 09107 Mota de Judios, Burgos, Spain.

Sonnet 21: On the Way to Carrión de los Condes

June 18, 2018—19 km (11.8 mi.)

We've gotten used to the morning routine
Of filling our camel bags with water.
We coat our faces and arms with sunscreen,
And open surface at the shirt's collar.

All equipped with adequate protection,
We leave in search of our next escapade.
At the fork, we choose the right direction,
With branches that contribute welcomed shade.

We come upon what looks like a ghost town
And follow the brown signs to the café.[1]
Through a green archway, paradise is found;
A garden where creatures and pilgrims play.

Warmly greeted by the donkey and ducks,
Only the grey goose is running amok!

---

1. Albergue Amanecer, calle Francesa, 1, 34447 Villarmentero de Campos, Palencia, Spain.

Sonnet 22: On the Way to Ledigos

June 19, 2018 23 km (14.3 mi)

We stop for provisions and directions.
The vendor explains the next town is far.
Only one stop between destinations,
And a pledged pilgrim doesn't drive a car.

We begin the long stretch under the shade
That soon recedes exposing beams of light,
A silent section of a joint crusade,
A true assessment of internal might.

We walk for seventeen kilometers
Through fields, over gravel, under the sun—
A challenge for the highest achiever,
Indeed demanding for the average one.

Just when we think there is no end in sight,
We see rooftops[1] and know we'll be alright.

---

1. Brierley, *A Pilgrim's Guide*, 160. "Rooftops" refers to the Village of Calzadilla de la Cueza.

6

Castilla y León (León)

Sonnet 23: On the Way to El Burgo Ranero

June 20, 2018—32 km (20.0 mi.)

We barely finish twenty miles today.
It's been by far our most exhausting task.
Though overhanging boughs demark the way,
Our growing aches and pains are hard to mask.

Most of our new Camino friends are gone,
Completing some components of the tour.
The rest, we have failed to see since dawn,
The pathways grow increasingly unsure.

Adjacent roadway edges well defined.
With bushes of yellow fragrant flowers,[1]
Plentiful, and to each of our senses kind,
Comforting us during peak walking hours.

The last stretch is always the most demanding,
But what counts is that we are still standing.

---

1 50. Annandale, *"Spanish-Broom,"* 58. "Yellow fragrant flowers," refers to a flower bush called the Spanish-Broom.

Sonnet 24: On the Way to Mansilla Mayor

June 21, 2018—22 km (13.7 mi.)

The walk continues under the maples,
Yet sunlight places shade upon the fields.
The subtle afternoon breeze at times enables
With the desired cooler temps, it yields.

We look forward to our daily snack breaks
At tempting eateries[1] along the way.
Stocked with egg tortillas[2] and homemade cakes,
We find it's hard to snub a sweet display.

Exhausted, we reach our bed and breakfast.[3]
Our gracious host bestows a warm greeting
And he insists we wine and dine with guests—
A feast we are grateful to be eating.

We finish our day with a soccer match[4]
Since the earlier game we could not catch.

1. Bar Restaurant Piedras Blancas 2, Lugar Reliegos, 1018, 24339 Leon, León, Spain.

2. Seneviratne, *Gluten-Free for Good*, 141. A traditional Spanish dish made in a skillet, with its primary ingredients being potatoes, eggs, olive oil, garlic and onions. I was a little skeptical when a local told us the best tortillas were at El Puntido. We stopped there on the way to Castrojeriz (Sonnet 19). It turned out to be the best tortilla I had on the pilgrimage. Mesón Albergue El Puntido 6, Calle la Iglesia, 09227 Hontanas, Burgos, Spain. https://www.puntido.com/

3. Guest House Joaco Travesia Padre Llorente 1, Mansilla Mayor, Mansilla De Las Mulas, Castilla y León, Spain, 24217. http://casajoaco.com/

4. 2018 FIFA World Cup, June 14–July 15, Fédération Internationale de Football.

Sonnet 25: On the Way to León

June 22, 2018—16 km (10 mi.)

We are met by imposing Roman walls.[1]
Through tangles of winding medieval streets,
We reach the plaza lined with vendor stalls
With a varied selection of good eats.

We arrive to celebrate with locals
The fiestas of both Saint John and Peter,[2]
A venue for all talented hopefuls
And destination for the staunch believer.

We settle into our rustic lodge[3]
In the famed city for a three-day stay.
Attracted to the festive noise barrage.
We join and watch the passing party sway.

We enjoy fireworks that light up the sky,
Reminiscent of the Fourth of July.

1. Brierley, *A Pilgrim's Guide*, 180.

2. Brierley, *A Pilgrim's Guide*, 180. "The fiestas of both Saints John and Peter," take place June 21—30.

3. Hotel La Posada Regia, Calle Regidores, 9–11, 24003 León, Spain. Http:// https://www.regialeon.com/

Sonnet 26: León

June 23, 2018

A horizon of terra cotta tiles
Interrupted by the cathedral[1] spires[2]—
A sight that can be seen for several miles.
The house of light, everyone admires.

Contemplating in quiet reverence,
All believers and agnostics alike
Are awestruck by the blissful elegance
Of the rose window's[3] gentle play of light.

Its comforting cooler temperatures
Provide respite from exterior heat,
Allowing longer gazes heavenwards,
Making all other noon plans obsolete.

I'm not exactly sure how much time was spent
Because self-reflection was my intent.

---

1. Brierley, *A Pilgrim's Guide,* 186. Santa María de León is a thirteenth century Gothic Cathedral. Plaza Regla, s/n, 24003 León, Spain. http://https://www.catedraldeleon.org/

2. Steves, *Spain 2017*, 301. The cathedral spires are an exterior decorative architectural element placed on top of the sructure's towers.

3. Steves, *Spain 2017*, 302. The large Gothic style wheel-shaped "rose window" is made of prismatic stained glass and features an image of the Virgin Mary at its center.

Sonnet 27: On the Way to Villadangos del Páramo

June 25, 2018—20 km (12.4 mi.)

The days are getting warmer and longer.
We leave before dawn to avoid the heat
To join the pilgrim queue that's much stronger.
All focus on the same goal to complete.

We choose the path parallel the highway
In favor of a shorter-distance stroll
That is quite distracting, to our dismay,
And disruptive to our hike as a whole.

As is customary on the dirt track,
We meet and chitchat with fellow hikers.
Distracted, we have a little setback:
One more unintended detour transpires.

At last we pinpoint our course mistake
Embarrassed for the repeat we must make.

Sonnet 28: On the Way to Astorga

June 26, 2018—26 km (16.2 mi.)

We wake to a pleasant and cool a.m.
The sun by inches slowly starts to rise.
It sparkles over the cornfields like a gem.
A sight that truly pleases pilgrim's eyes.

And still degrees begin their cyclic climb,
Compounding more this proven rough terrain.
As predicted the summer at its prime
The combo leaves us feeling rather drained.

Each step is painful on this rocky course
Devoid of shade and muted all throughout.
A place where water is a precious source
And creates questions in the most devout.

The heavens darken fueling thunderous bolts.
We locate shelter from alarming jolts.

Sonnet 29: On the Way to Rabanal del Camino

June 27, 2018—20 km (12.4 mi.)

Embellished paths with purple English blooms
Resemble flawless lettercard vignettes.
Anointed with an herbal spiced perfume,
The weary traveler some malaise forgets.

We are told of a Gregorian chant
At a small church[1] in the center of town.
Benedictine Monks sing songs that enchant
And welcome believers from all around.

At dusk the set of sacred songs recedes
And on our way down, we spot a good friend.
To see her was miraculous indeed,
For it is her devotion we commend.

We do a little bit of catching up
And make arrangements for a follow up.

---

1. Brierley, *A Pilgrim's Guide*, 206–7. Benedictine Monastery San Salvador del Monte Irago, Calle Calvario 6 E, 24722 Rabanal del Camino. Https://monteirago.org/

Sonnet 30: On the Way to Molinaseca

June 28, 2018—25 km (15.5 mi.)

The steep climb through the charming hillside place[1]
Provides a hint of early morn's ascent.
The challenge of the day's extended race
Is softened by the mountain's fresh dew scent.

Lost in thought and mountain views,
We are unaware how much time has lapsed.
Upon us reaching nature's deepest hues,
We realize we have arrived at last.

Pilgrims converge at the Cruz de Ferro,[2]
A plain but quite symbolic iron cross,
Pointing to the heavens like an arrow.
Stones are placed for a blessing or a loss.

A feeling of elation fills the space.
All spontaneously smile and embrace!

---

1. Brierley, *A Pilgrim's Guide*, 207. "Hillside place" refers to Rabanal del Camino.

2. Brierley, *A Pilgrim's Guide,* 210.

Sonnet 31: On the Way to Villafranca del Bierzo

June 29, 2018—27 km (16.8 mi.)

The region's cherry season at its peak,
Each branch drooping from the weight of its fruit.
We pick some for a taste of the unique
And sneak off to enjoy our tasty loot.

On the hill, the Castle of the Templars[1]
With imposing stone walls and watchtowers.
An order whose life calling is stellar
And has unparalleled earthly powers.

Touring the castle grounds sets us off course,
And we are warned of an impending storm
That threatens to hit the region with force.
The skies slowly darken and grey clouds form.

We arrive late into the evening hours
To a quaint village[2] under rain showers.

---

1. Brierley, *A Pilgrim's Guide*, 217. Castle of the Templars, Av. el Castillo, s/n, 24400 Ponferrada, León, Spain. Https://castillodelostemplarios.com/

2. Brierley, *A Pilgrim's Guide*, 222. "Quaint village" refers to Villafranca del Bierzo.

Sonnet 32: On the Way to Las Herrerías

June 30, 2018—20 km (12.4 mi.)

Arising to another splendid sight
Of hillside wine estates and country homes.
Enveloped under the moon's subtle light,
A province[1] where local farmers roam.

We leave with added dread of certain rain:
Again the grey expanse resounds and roars.
No day on the Camino is mundane,
Especially when spending time outdoors.

A soft and steady drip begins to fall,
Quickly turning into angled showers.
It is no surprise to any at all
When the deluge goes on for several hours.

Within minutes, we are completely soaked.
It never ceases raining like we hoped.

---

1. Brierley, *A Pilgrim's Guide, 222.* "Quaint village" refers to Villafranca
del Bierzo.

7

Galicia (Lugo)

Sonnet 33: On the Way to Triacastela

July 1, 2018 29 km (18.0 mi.)

We climb a dense forest of mossy trees
Over slippery paths of solid rock.
The steep ascent is all everyone sees
Through the rays of sun the leaves fail to block.

The clanging cowbells can be heard nearby
And burbles from the deep ravine below.[1]
We watch a herd of stately cows pass by
Returning home from grazing the meadow.

We spot a good friend on the mountainside
Who's been a steady presence in our quest.
She has been a kind of spiritual guide,
More so than either of us would have guessed.

Our departure is somewhat bittersweet
Since, together, we won't finish this feat.

---

1. "Deep ravine below," refers to the Mazaco River or Río Mazaco.

Sonnet 34: On the Way to Sarria

July 2, 2018—22 km (13.7 mi.)

The woodland resembles a cloud forest,
Where ferns are plentiful and grow with ease.
The blooms, the envy of every florist,
And the cool, damp shade can't help but appease.

Amid this enchantment, we find an inn.
Attended by a sole obliging host,
Who too kindly invites us to come in
Before exploring other fabled posts.

A group of children joined some days ago,
Bestowing their contagious youthful will.
Enjoying tunes and setting hearts aglow,
And learning classic lessons that instill.

We laugh at silly jests at every turn
And wonder if one day they will return.

Sonnet 35: On the Way to Portomarín

July 3, 2018—24 km (15 mi.)

Busloads of fresh new pilgrims pass us by,
Racing as we once had to the finish.
None say buen camino or even hi,
But their vast numbers quickly diminish.

Moving steadily beyond the gridlock,
We are able to continue our stride
And run into cows of a select stock[1]
That carry their sculptural horns with pride.

We arrive at a pristine lakefront town[2]
With staggered white buildings and hilltop church[3]
And a long bridge in shades of grey and brown,
Where the sleepy town and calm lakeshore merge.

We watch the sunset over the water,
The pilgrim dad with his pilgrim daughter.

---

1. Meakin, *Galicia, The Switzerland of Spain*, 212—14. The Gallegan Cow is a breed of cattle found in Galicia, Spain and is distinguished by its long sculptural horns.

2. Brierley, *A Pilgrim's Guide*, 251-52. "Pristine lakefront town" refers to Portomarín, Spain.

3. Brierley, *A Pilgrim's Guide*, 252. Iglesia de San Juan, 27170 Portomarín, Lugo, Spain. http://www.concellodeportomarin.es/

Sonnet 36: On the Way to Palas de Rei

July 4, 2018—24 km (15 mi.)

As hundreds join a single western route,
We each look forward to the final mile.
The end of an all-terrain commute,
We vanish into one expanding file.

The parish[1] bells resound, announcing mass.
Entranced by lyric sounds of vocal chords,
The faithful in the central nave amass
To hear the spoken word of the Lord.

The quest of self-reflection soon concludes
And marks the start of other life pursuits,
The future goal we seek for now eludes,
But our hearts and minds are more acute.

The day ends with a show we want to see,
And simple sweet desserts and herbal tea.

1. Parroquia de San Tirso de Palas de Rei, Rúa Cruceiro, 1, 27200 Palas de Rei, Lugo, Spain.

8

Galicia (La Coruña)

Sonnet 37: On the Way to Arzúa

July 5, 2018 29 km (18.0 mi.)

We let ourselves be carried by the crowd
Through heavily worn ancient woodland tracks.
Encircling all in an evergreen shroud,
The blue barely visible through the cracks.

We enter a quaint twelfth-century shrine,[1]
Home to a sixteenth-century fresco.
Whose figures are difficult to define,
But a treasure for this tiny pueblo.[2]

Pilgrims flood the small delicate structure
In search of a coveted passport stamp.
But fail to notice the unique feature
Of this centuries-old lime plaster craft.

We take a moment and admire the art:
An unpretentious piece painted with heart.

1. Iglesia de Santa María de Leboreiro, 15809 O Leboreiro, A Coruña, Spain.
2. "Pueblo" refers to the hamlet of O Leboreiro in Melide (A Coruña Province)

Sonnet 38: On the Way to Santiago de Compostela

July 6, 2018—37 km (23 mi.)

The final stage begins before first dawn,
And watch the sunrise gleam above the mount.
We think of hiking friends we made, now gone—
So many, it is difficult to count.

There through the street, that opens to the square,
A house of worship[1] of exquisite grace.
An architectural feat that's quite rare,
For some, its setting is the chosen place.

Both guests and faithful flood the sacred hall,
To listen and partake in joyful praise.
And bathe in incense clouds and heed the call
On the Almighty, so many wish to gaze.

At close of service, we could not believe:
Our friend! No better gift could we receive.

---

1. Cathedral of Santiago de Compostela Praza do Obradoiro, s/n, 15704 Santiago de Compostela, A Coruña, Spain. Http://catedraldesantiago.es/

Sonnet 39: On the Way to Finisterre

July 7, 2018

A morning shuttle takes us furthest west,
Toward the zero kilo waymarked base.[1]
A major milestone of a lifelong quest,
The impulse to continue grows apace.

The verdant land of the Atlantic coast,
At one time settled by a Celtic tribe;[2]
The now location of a lighthouse post,[3]
A scene, at best a picture can describe.

A final stop, a chapel[4] marred by fire.
With patience, hand restored by skillful folk.
A problem that appeared immensely dire,
To salvage items lost by flames and smoke.

Reluctant to enter airport gates,
Encouraged by the calling that awaits!

1. Zero-kilometer marker at Cape Finisterre or Cabo Fisterra—the end of the Way of St. James.

2. Brierley, *A Pilgrim's Guide*, 30.

3. Cape Finisterre Lighthouse, Cabo Fisterra, s/n, 15155 Fisterra, A Coruña, Spain. https://www.concellofisterra.com

4. Virxe da Barca Sanctuary, Lugar Virxe Barca, 1G, 15124, A Coruña, Spain.

Conclusion

"THANK YOU."

Hearing the gratitude and appreciation in my father's voice as we disembarked at LAX brought tears to my eyes. In that quiet moment, I realized the gift I had been given: a father-daughter bond stronger than either of us could have imagined, forged during this life-changing adventure along the Camino, through resilience, perseverance, and love.

Months later, I am happy to say the lessons I learned traveling the Camino de Santiago reappear daily in my life, allowing me opportunities to act with empathy and courage in unexpected ways. I can also understand how, by writing about my excursion in these sonnets, I have created a metaphor about my journey as a lifelong physical and spiritual traveler.

My father and I are currently deciding on our next destination. I can't wait to see what unfolds!

It is worth noting that a Compostela Holy Year or Año Xacobeo[1] is upon us, the day in which the feast of the Apostle Saint James the Great falls on a Sunday. In addition to a greater number of festivities and visitors—more than a quarter million—devout pilgrims from all over the world can follow steps to plenary indulgence, the Catholic tradition of completely absolving sins. The last feast occurred in 2010, the next will be July 25, 2021, and we will not see another until 2027. Therefore, if you would like to join the ranks of some famous pilgrims, like Steven Hawking, Shirley

1. Steves, *Spain 2017*, 252.

MacLaine, and Anthony Quinn, or feel a pressing need to absolve your sins, the year of the jubilee may be just what you have been waiting for!

Packing Essentials

I DID A LOT of research and read countless backpack reviews, but ultimately I found my backpack in an outdoor specialty store. I visited the store three times, gauged the practicality of the numerous designs, spoke with several employees, and was measured and fitted with backpacks of various sizes. I carried my final choice around the store for over an hour with an additional 10 lb. weight and to my surprise, no discomfort—SOLD!

In addition to the backpack's numerous features, some more valuable to me than others, I chose a bright aqua-colored backpack that my dad would be able to spot from a distance.

Clothing

- ☐ Two long-sleeved, moisture-wicking, rapid-evaporation, and UPF 40 sun-protection blouses
- ☐ Two short-sleeved, moisture-wicking T-shirts
- ☐ Two moisture-wicking camisoles (for layering in inclement weather)
- ☐ Two rapid-evaporation walking pants
- ☐ Two pairs of wool socks
- ☐ Three pairs of silk socks (to wear as liners underneath the wool socks)

Packing Essentials

- [ ] One moisture-wicking cap
- [ ] One moisture-wicking gaiter
- [ ] Four quick-dry underwear
- [ ] One moisture-wicking, zippered hoodie with thumbholes (The thumbholes allow the sleeves to protect the tops of your hands from the sun when using walking poles.)
- [ ] One pair of waterproof hiking shoes
- [ ] One pair of Crocs-style shoes
- [ ] Rain poncho
- [ ] One travel clothesline

Hiking Gear

- [ ] A pair of light, adjustable walking poles
- [ ] A small emergency kit (Pharmacies along the Camino specialize in every kind of walking issue.)
- [ ] One hiking backpack with CamelBak-type water bag
- [ ] One waterproof backpack rain cover
- [ ] Small flashlight

Electronics

- [ ] One cellphone (Bring a phone that takes excellent pictures, has plenty of space, is large enough to work on your social media, and is reliable for connecting to maps and services in case of an emergency)
- [ ] Charger
- [ ] Continental plug adapter

Documents

- ☐ Passport from country of origin
- ☐ Pilgrim Passport
- ☐ Identification: driver, student, hostel, etc.
- ☐ *A Pilgrim's Guide to the Camino de Santiago* by John Brierley (or guide of your choice)
- ☐ One small notebook
- ☐ One tiny pen

Toiletries

- ☐ One travel soap leaves pack (Bathrooms were clean but didn't always have hand soap, and these were very light to carry.)
- ☐ One travel detergent
- ☐ One travel toilet paper roll
- ☐ Facial tissue
- ☐ One pack of hand wipes
- ☐ Small toothpaste
- ☐ Toothbrush
- ☐ Dental floss
- ☐ Medications
- ☐ One small, elongated travel towel (I used this to dry my face and hands, wrap around my nose and mouth, and cover up the back of my neck)

Recommended

- ☐ Bring something to share (I always travel with a couple dozen rose pins from my city. I give them to people with whom I make a positive connection.)

- ☐ Social networker's business cards (You do not want to miss an opportunity to stay in touch with someone wonderful, with whom you only connected briefly.)

- ☐ Burden Stone to place at the base of the Cruz de Ferro (Sonnets 2 and 30.)

Small Hotel Perks

I chose small hotels purposely, for their amenities. Small hotels often provide their guests with a number of useful items such as towels, body soap, shampoo, conditioner, loofahs, sponges, toothpaste, toothbrush, body lotion, razors. We only used what we needed and took any half-used items with us so as to not create waste. This saved us from carrying towels and large bottles.

Bibliography

Annandale, Charles, ed. *The New Cabinet Cyclopædia and Treasury of Knowledge: A Handy Book of Reference for all Readers*. Philadelphia: The Gebbie, 1900.

Brierley, John. *A Pilgrim's Guide to the Camino de Santiago: St. Jean-Roncesvalles-Santiago*, 14th ed. Forres, Scotland: Camino Guides, 2017.

Dearborn, Mary V. *Ernest Hemingway: A Biography*. New York: Knopf, 2017.

Frayer, Lauren, et al. *Essential Spain 2019*. Edited by Jacinta O'Halloran et al. 2nd ed. El Segundo, CA: Fodor's Travel, 2019.

Ham, Anthony, et al. *Lonely Planet Spain: Travel Guide*. Carlton, Australia: Lonely Planet, 2016.

Kurlansky, Mark. *The Basque History of the World*. New York: Penguin, 1999.

Marsh, Terry. *Michelin Green Guide: French Atlantic Coast; Travel Guide*. Boulogne-Billancourt, France: Michelin Travel Partner, 2016.

Meakin, Annette M. B. *Galicia, The Switzerland of Spain*. London: Methuen & Co., 1909.

Paterson, M. Linda. *The World of the Troubadours: Medieval Occitan Society. c1100–c.1300*. Cambridge: Cambridge University Press, 1993.

Seneviratne, Samantha. *Gluten-Free for Good: Simple, Wholesome Recipes Made from Scratch*. New York: Clarkson Potter, 2016.

Steves, Rick. *Paris*, Berkeley, CA: Avalon Travel, 2008.

———. *Spain*, Berkeley, CA: Avalon Travel, 2016.

———. *Spain*, Berkeley, CA: Avalon Travel, 2017.

Szwed, John. *Billie Holiday: The Musician and the Myth*. New York: Penguin, 2015.

Wallace, Tim. "The Guatemala Volcano Eruption: Before and After a Deadly Pyroclastic Flow." *New York Times*, June 7, 2018. https://www.nytimes.com/interactive/2018/06/07/world/americas/guatemala-volcano-eruption.html.

Wanamaker, Marc. *Hollywood: 1940–2008*. San Francisco: Arcadia, 2009.

Index

Index

Index

www.ingramcontent.com/pod-product-compliance
Lightning Source LLC
LaVergne TN
LVHW021616080426
835510LV00019B/2601